# Outlaws – Primary Source Edition

## Nancy Cunard

# OUTLAWS

# OUTLAWS

BY

NANCY CUNARD

LONDON
ELKIN MATHEWS, CORK STREET
MCMXXI

*The thanks of the Author are due to the Editors of " The English Review," " The New Age," and " Wheels," for kind permission to reprint certain poems in this volume.*

# CONTENTS

# 6    CONTENTS

# OUTLAWS

## I

THERE is a curious legend of two lovers
That thrills within the heart of every man ;
Ghostly they are, yet living, and the span
Allotted them by fate no end discovers.
There was a man, adventurous and free,
Evil of soul, grown into league with hell,
Loved by a woman that no fear might quell ;
Their lives rose as the waves grow out at sea.
Wild as the glory of a desert lion,
Dark as the sombre magnitude of death,
Heavy with memories as a storm that saith
Aloud its toll of corpses. . . . Cruel iron
Lay as a heart within this man, yet still
She followed him ; he held her to his will.

## II

Her heart held many musics ; many songs
Shone like fair crystals in her tenderness,
And all her longing was for happiness ;
Yet love was darkened by her lover's wrongs

And wild unlawful piracies, though he
Worshipped with passion, elemental flame
That burns, consuming self ; the soul untame
Burnt in each freely.  They shall never see
The shuddering brinks behind them, never know
The perilous moments nor the cruel hour
When death strove for them ; but with haunted eyes
Speed to infinity, while all this slow
World's musing chronicle records the power
That dwelt in their strange love that never dies.

### III

And so they wandered through life's haunted rooms,
Each other's heart laid bare to each, and hid
In secrecy from all the rest, amid
Their happiness and tragedies and glooms.
Life drew its ghosts around them, and on walls
Lingered strange shadows that were more than life
In their deep artifice.  A trenchant knife
Above them hung, the knife that never falls
But trembles in its warning.  Voices came
From out the elements, from sea and fire
To lead them on ; they conquered all desire
With passion ever-new.  Adventure's flame
Was sealed upon their souls that did aspire
And reached up to the transient face of fame.

## IV

Outlawed, aloof, like thunderclouds they sped
Over the restless breathing of the sea ;
And those around shook at their liberty,
And trembled at their power.  Alone the dead
Were free from these magicians' modern charms
That vaunted lawlessness and love and pleasure :
Drawing the brave into a swifter measure,
Leading the brave into the life that harms
All but its strange initiate.  Their crimes
Sped down the course of nature unrestrained.
While others fell they conquered, careful, trained,
Well practised in their art ; yet there were times
Most near to death—then she, who loved so well,
Saved him, and straightway gave her soul to hell.

## V

Love was too little for him, fate too strong,
And took in payment from him folly's toll ;
And yet she loved him with a patience long,
And eyes kept clear wherewith to view the soul,
The shaking battlefield that nourished him
And filled with tempests the proud tortured eyes
That mirrored her reflected love, yet grim,
Brooding remained ; as by a fire that dies

Sits an impenitent with ravenous crimes
That will not cry aloud nor mercy seek,
Through haunted midnights sped with cruel
    chimes,
Locked in himself—till finally the sleek
Pale face of morning puts to flight the dim,
Mad, raving, windy ghosts that follow him.


VI


Flayed souls that flee before a shivering wind
Out to the dark horizons of the sea ;
Eternal wanderers that may never be
Stilled by the touch of death.  A pirate's mind
Steers their black ships ; his soul makes full their
    sails
With the wild winds of courage, and the waves
Daily grow great between them over graves
Of others not so free.  When daylight fails
They may be seen alongside each to each,
Two lovers passionate of life and stress,
Stepped from the lands of hell to earth above :
A man that failed with heaven in his reach,
And she, that should have crowned a king, no
    less,
Yet then as now held but her crown of love.

## VII

One thinks to hear them crying in the wind :
" Life was so bitter to us—but we chose
The living, stressful moments from this close
Denying, grey existence.  If we sinned
We bear our joys and crimes with equal heart,
And punishment is nothing.  We have known
All sweet and sharp adventures, and are grown
Heroic-hard with life.  You cannot part
Our twin minds from each other, and we sail
Proud and forever on the clutching sea,
Grown element again ;  the heaven's breath
Makes clear our souls with space ; life does not fail
As we have used it.". . . They shall ever be ;
Summer has set upon them but not death.

# AND IF THE END BE NOW?...

THE rooms are empty and the streets are bare,
No lovers meet at midnight under stars,
And the past pleasures of congenial hours
Forgotten lie ; yet now these flowers that fade
Once dressed the gardens with a gay delight.
Ah, patiently we must grow friends with grey,
Put out of mind the colour of the flame
And the triumphant songs of inspiration ;
Obliterate adventure, memory.
The silence of desertion has begun
And the slow madness of annihilation ;
Think you we can be friends with nothingness
And make a song out of an empty hour ?
Somewhere the world has changed, the sun slipped
    round
To lands antipodean, leaving us
Like wandering dreamers in long corridors
That may not be got through, a circular maze
That guards the promised land of Never More ;
Alone, alone we wander with our dream—
Ah, I have felt remote before to-night,
As if some word had drifted down from God
To warn my soul of the eventual end

And the completed solitude to be.
I have felt married to eternity,
Already bade farewell to things and days,
And seen their transmutation into ghosts
That gravely intimate the parting sign—
And if the end be now have I known all?
Let us examine conscience' hieroglyph . . .
The adolescent love of mysticism,
Followed by bitter sceptic pride and scorn
Of what life seemed to give, gave into hands
Too frail to hold, looked into eyes too veiled
With youthful sorrows to let comfort in.
And there was independence, solemnly
Scheming to build the tower impregnable
That should throw shadow over half the earth;
And fortitude and courage, like wild steeds
They raved and never could be brought to rein,
And so made havoc, vainly wasting strength
Till their nobility was lost indeed.
Love came along and seemed the conqueror
That should set right the world, proclaiming
    justice
With many promises of inspiration
And a high creed of generosity;
(Of all religions Love the proudest is,
And will not be gainsaid, but though eternal,
By its own flame it fades, consuming us).

There have been other martyrs on this wheel
That turns to-day before me : introspection,
And that fanatic, self-analysis,
With soul archaic as the early saint
That knelt with grace to clasp the cross and
    death ;
But oh, my saint dies not ! and glories still
Turning the knife each day in painful wounds
With self-infliction growing ever deeper. . . .
Yet there are moods when I can plumb the world
And seem to tell the purpose of the stars,
Grasp at the palm of fate, transcending earth.
This is the tranquil mood of certainty
That lies above us as the distant sunset.

      .     .     .     .     .

After the beat of sorrow's passionate hands
Came melancholy with a gesture calm ;
And in her motion was the breath of sleep
And musing poetry, to soothe despair ;
And here time seemed to turn a gentle hermit
Putting aside the weary web of stress ;
Akin with nature, merging into autumn
With a long pause as if eternal—Then
The human world obtrudes, the daily tides
Of feverish events surge up again
And to a further controversy beckon.

      .     .     .     .     .

My hands are empty now, my heart as void
Of all emotions as a timeless dawn
When the last stars are lost, before some day
Has made complete actuality of hours.
Now close the doors and let the pulse of earth
Slip unperceived to final quietude,
For life has taken much in giving much—
In that shall lie the balance of the end.

# MOON

Slowly the moon grows larger, I can see
The real solitude to be to-night,
And the vain longing of a muted heart
As when two lovers have been long asunder.
She counts the minutes, pale and silently
Draws nearer to the sea ; the little waves
Become all great with longing, wreath'd with foam ;
Already a long stairway from the sky
Descending slowly rests upon the earth,
And thoughts, like spirits, on it come and go.

   .    .    .    .    .    .

Oh puissant unattainable white moon,
My soul has taken pause, saluting thee.

# THE SONNET OF HAPPINESS

OVER the City lie the gathered stars,
The streets are holy in their emptiness
As I go with you, great with happiness.
We have inherited the strength of Mars
And the proud love of Venus ; we are free !
Let us make good our freedom, for we are wise
And bravely passionate ; this enterprise
Shall long endure like a fine ship at sea.
To-night we'll have no melodrama, tears,
Or sudden partings of dissatisfaction,
No wavering purpose or unglorious action,
No hesitation or uncertain fears ;
But in a solitude of silence Grecian
Shall know the plenitude of life's completion.

I

WHAT is this cry for toys ? you've had them all ;
This clamouring for lovers ? take your choice :
Outgrown and senseless dolls with timid voice,
Like marionettes unstrung they can but fall
Into your merciful hands, your tender grasp
That pities them and tidies up their tears ;
The while you wince, yet put away their fears,
Their sorrows soothe, their anguished hands un-
    clasp.
For they have sunk all pride in commonness,
Lost the contumely look, the daily speech ;
Lie at your feet—bend down, let fingers reach
An ultimate kiss to them—forgetfulness . . .
And then maybe your sorrows, each by each,
Will pardon beg for you, end your distress.

## II

YET when the night draws on, you long for arms,
Arms to enfold, becalm your soul away,
Gestures to quell, a voice that says : " To-day
Is a spent nightmare, rest you from alarms
And be unharassed ; you have done with fear
For a short season and shall claim reward,
That share of victory that has been stored
For you in well-kept sequence, costing dear."
And in the sunset stillness of that hour
Maybe you'll dream of lying down with Death,
Your ultimate lover ; but your soul and breath
Must first be parted by that unknown power
Of time or fate, whatever name is given
To that strange path that's said to lead to heaven.

# PRAISE

I LOVE the gesture of your open hands
Expounding things : the blinding streak of fire
That lights the voice of your imagination.
I love your laugh and all its cadences,
The tempests of your speech, the flaming words
Of wisdom, all the agile nimble thoughts
That seethe and simmer in your smiling brain ;
The oratory of truths you have declaimed,
The conquest of the difficult and dark
Obstructions laid by life along your way.
You have not fallen, failed nor faltered once,
Nor looked behind in doubt, but undismayed
Have faced the sun.  In your dark eyes I see
The promises of miracles, the lure
Of brilliant new horizons, hopes found good,
And dreams to make the gods rejoice and sing.

You are an army flushed with conquered wines,
Feasting on luxury and new delight—
You are the king of joy, the world is tamed
And spread before you in magnificence ;
The subtle and the sensuous are your slaves,
And all the seven wonders now made clear

Delivered you as prize.  I will stand by
And look into a corner of your heart
To see if you are happy, if your crown
Be not of gold too heavy, whether pain
Shall be excluded from this great new rule,
And all the sorrows and incertitudes
Put to the torture they have merited.
I think that you will now make free our days,
And conquer time ; you shall not know defeat.

For you are priest of Possibility,
Hero of new-discovered continents,
Pure as the endless sea, spirit of love
Created from the essences of stars
And the pulsating powers of elements ;
There are no bounds nor limits to your speed,
No mountain huge enough to crush your heart,
Nothing to kill the genius of your soul.

# THE LOVERS

HUNDREDS of lovers there have been,
  Princes and clowns and fools ;
Mighty, timid, low, obscene,
And some whose hearts were never clean
  Who set aside all rules.

Dark lovers from the burning lands,
  And giants from the plain,
And some with wicked cruel hands,
And some God made and understands,
  And more that Death has slain.

Pale boys too beautiful to live,
  Too wild and proud and young,
With eager eyes and hearts that give
A love this life cannot forgive
  And sends its snakes among.

And some that lied and stole and swore
  To fill the world with vice,
Who fought each other and made war
Till Fate came knocking at the door
  And made them pay the price.

Strange subtlety, sweet happiness
  Some gave and others took !
Yet lovers all, who once did bless
The love that leads men to distress
  And marks with bitter look.

Now Death has stolen all away,
  And bade them love and kiss
Pale shadows of a yesterday,
With empty hands and hearts that sway
  In darker worlds than this.

# WHEELS

I SOMETIMES think that all our thoughts are wheels,
Rolling forever through a painted world :
Moved by the cunning of a thousand clowns
Dressed paper-wise, with blatant rounded masks,
That take their multi-coloured caravans
From place to place, and act and leap and sing,
Catching the spinning hoops when cymbals clash.
And one is dressed as Fate, and one as Death ;
The rest that represent Love, Joy and Sin,
Join hands in solemn stage-learnt ecstasy,
While Folly beats a drum with golden pegs,
And mocks that shrouded jester called Despair.
The dwarfs and other curious satellites,
Voluptuous-mouthed, with slyly pointed steps
Strut in the circus while the people stare.
And some have sober faces white with chalk
And roll the heavy wheels all through the streets
Of sleeping hearts, with ponderance and noise
Like weary armies on a solemn march.
Now in the scented gardens of the Night
Where we are scattered like a pack of cards,
Our words are turned to spokes that thoughts may
    roll,

And form a ringing chain around the world,
(Itself a fabulous wheel controlled by Time
Over the slow incline of centuries.)
So dreams and prayers, and feelings born of sleep,
As well as all the sun-gilt pageantry
Made out of summer breezes and hot noons,
Are in the great revolving of the spheres
Under the trampling of their chariot wheels.

# ZEPPELINS

I SAW the people climbing up the street
Maddened with war and strength and thought to
    kill ;
And after followed Death, who held with skill
His torn rags royally, and stamped his feet.

The fires flamed up and burnt the serried town,
Most where the sadder, poorer houses were ;
Death followed with proud feet and smiling stare,
And the mad crowds ran madly up and down.

And many died and hid in unfound places
In the black ruins of the frenzied night ;
And Death still followed in his surplice, white
And streaked in imitation of their faces.

    .     .     .     .     .     .

But in the morning men began again
To mock Death following in bitter pain.

# THE LAST OF PIERROT

PIERROT again on octaves strums around,
(Octaves his only meaning, speech and measure,)
White, wasted, wanton fool that kisses pleasure
Thinking with love's glass knife to stab the ground
And draw life-blood from out his painted heart ;
Forgetting that its texture is but paper,
More fragile frills than gossamer or vapour,
A ribbon, tied with eighteenth-century art.

He sits and shivers on a tattered stool,
Hearing the cold grind out the endless breath
From saddened shadows : " Sober now," he saith,
" The cards lie upwards on the useless pool,
The drums are filled with blood and wine and lead,
Carnaval buried long, and Pierrot dead."

# SONNET

THIS is no time for prayers or words or song ;
With folded hands we sit and slowly stare,
The world's old wheels go round, and like a fair
The clowns and peepshows ever pass along.
Our brains are dumb with cold and worn with strife,
And every day has lingered on our faces,
Marking its usual course and weary paces
With cruel cunning care and sober knife.
Fate, like a sculptor working with great tools,
Now moulds his genius into clever ways ;
Our souls are cut and torn all for his praise
When his great masterpiece is praised by fools ;
But Death has beaten him, and takes the pride
From the strong hands that held us till we died.

# WAR

AND yet we live while others die for us ;
Live in the glory of sweet summer, still
Knowing not death, but knowing that life will
Be merciless to them—and so to us.
Blood lies too rich on many battlefields,
Too many crowns are made for solemn sorrow ;
We rise from weeping, and the cruel morrow
Has nought, but to a further sorrow yields.
No god is yet arisen, who with fair
Firm judgment shall arrest this course of war
And make destruction cease ; say : " Nature's law
Too long hath broken been." None yet may dare
Hold out a mighty hand, bid Death withdraw,
Or break the current of this world-despair.

## MONKERY!

Oh multitude of popish monkery,
Give up your praying, spare your incense now,
For God has long forgotten your faint hearts
And your long self-inflicted suffering.
Give over challenging the wicked world
To steal your contrite souls from sacrifice ;
This is no age of prophets, who with vows
Lived long in wildernesses, burnt at stake,
Or were translated into glorious heaven
Without the knowledgeable fear of death.
Put out the altar candles one by one,
Close down your sainted books and liturgies,
Untie the chaplets of your gathered beads,
And bow farewell to sanctity of church
(Recluseful ease wherein were spent your days).
This is a time of strife and war and death ;
Against all these no prayers of man prevail ;
But all the term of Time's impatience now
Is loosely rampant, and destruction comes
To burn and pillage what was long thought safe.
But when once more the passionate earth is bound
And quieted by plenitude of peace
There must arise a greater, truer life

Above the formula of mere religion ;
And as the ancient order passeth ever
Into the transmutation of the new,
So must all practices of former days
Sink in the silent whirlpool of the past.

# 1917

THE curtains of the sky are tightly drawn ;
As in a horrid sunken maze the sun
Is veiled with wickedness, and all the streets
Shine horribly and wanly at noontide.
Now all the precious greenery of trees,
Remaining deaf to the command of spring,
Is still imprisoned by late lagging time ;
And in the silence of the winter night
There are as yet no signs of moon or dawn ;
And in the minds of men there is no hope,
No spark of courage to foresee the end
Of the long-reigning period of this war.

While like the murmur of a thousand clocks
Wild apprehensions crowd into the days,
And force their weary fingers at our throats.
There is no use in putting on a mask
And crying " kamerad " to death and strife ;
There is no way to close our troubled hearts
To all the things that we have known before
(Yet then found loopholes to escape therefrom).
Each day a fever that's both new and old
Will come and struggle with our weariness.

And there will be no spring, no summer more
When the sweet smile of heaven rests on earth ;
No faith, nor enterprise.   Secretly still
We shall go slinking through the web of Time ;
And when the war is ended, glorious dreams
That have been planned and nurtured with our
    blood
(Conceived of faith in blind futurity)
Will float unseizable from our weak hands ;
And there will be no joy of road or sea,
No freedom of fresh countries and rich towns,
No glory in a peace that comes too late.

c

# PROMISE

HAD I a clearer brain, imagination,
A flowing pen, and better-ending rhymes,
A firmer heart devoid of hesitation,
Unbiassed happiness these troubled times,
With pleasure in this discontented life,
Forgetfulness of sorrow and of pain :
Triumphant victory over fear and strife,
Daring to look behind, and look again
Ahead for all the slowly coming days :
See nothing but the carnivals of peace,
Forget the dreams of death and other ways
Men have imagined for their own decrease—
I'd write a song to conquer all our tears
Lasting forever through the folding years.

# LAMENT

I AM an angry child's last broken toy,
Left over from the games of yesterday,
Forgotten in a corner, cast away
By the tired hands of some small peevish boy.

I am a broken idol of last year,
Once worshipped richly in a golden shrine,
A deathless god that nations called divine,
Yet found another whom they did prefer.

I am an exiled king without his crown,
A dying poet with a tattered mask,
A starving beggar who may nothing ask,
And a religion that has been cast down.

# MOOD

Smoke-stacks, coal-stacks, hay-stacks, slack,
Colourless, scentless, pointless, dull,
Railways, highways, roadways black,
Grantham, Birmingham, Leeds, and Hull.

Steamers, passengers, convoys, trains,
Merchandise travelling over the sea,
Smutty streets and factory lanes—
What can these ever mean to me ?

# THE KNAVE OF SPADES

You are the Knave of Spades ; I swear you are
No other personage, no other card
In any pack has that satanic eye.
You are the soul of highway robbery,
And you have nimbly mocked at all those toys,
Pistols and crossbones, horses, masks and skulls ;
For you have been too swift in every chase
And now you hover round forgotten gibbets,
Staring, and laugh.  Again you are a wild
Great stamping Tartar full of ecstasy ;
Your speech is suave, yet like a scimitar
Cleaves the white air with blazing irony.
I love you, Longhi's darkest lurking shadow,
Appearing suddenly, as quickly gone
Back to your eighteenth-century lagoons ;
I am not sure *you* weren't that famous snake
That is accused of having tempted Eve
With apple-talk ; (you knew how well to lie).
I hope that I shall never live to see
In your dark face the sign of any pain
Or any creeping sorrow that spoils pride ;
(The pride of devils that may never suffer).
I think you have been king of your desires,

First granting them, then turning them to dust ;
Weirwolf, enchanter, sometimes Harlequin,
A bitter Harlequin of curious moods
When midnight trembles and the West meets
    East . . .
God knows what more, but I prefer just now
To think of you as that same Knave of Spades,
A fiendish rebel with no heart ; and yet
You are my love, the witchcraft of my faith.

# PSALM

IT makes you blind and mad ; tears like a fire
Tears at the root of things, destroying all
Till the last flame is out, but love goes on.
Sometimes it gladdens you with valiancy,
Oh false fleet feeling that dies down too soon
Under the waters of reaction.  True,
Love is a thing you shall not do without,
Nor having, hold it ;  bitter salted bread,
Disguised like shameful poison at a feast ;
And those two brimming cups each side of you
Really contain the drunkenness of pain
And not the intoxicants of earthly wine.

You  may  not  spurn  this  unknown  hedge-row
      guest
That others jeer at, till he frightens them
With a thrown-off disguise ;  for love slips in
Behind you unawares.  Some call him life,
The cowards call him death, and close their eyes
Under the ardent passion-flames of pain.

Love has the brave in his especial care,
And leads them open-eyed through all the worlds

Of hell and heaven ; what wonder then if some
Go mad with climbing to such altitudes
Forgetting the descent ?   Heroes alone
Love takes for his unknown and ultimate ends,
And turns for them the thorns to passion-flowers
That never fade—immortalising love.

But dreary horny-handed fate sets out
Drawing the scattered back into the net ;
And when the racing of the mill is done,
If love has pardoned you, and pitied you,
Comes from the wreck a phœnix, and you've got—
Friendship, that topmost solitary star.

# PRAYER

Oꜱ God, make me incapable of prayer,
Too brave for supplication, too secure
To feel the taunt of danger ! Let my heart
Be tightened mightily to withstand pain,
And make me suffer singly, without loss.
Now let me bear alone the ageing world
On firmer shoulders than the giant Atlas.
Make me symbolic'ly iconoclast,
The ideal Antichrist, the Paradox.

# SIRENS

Your life—a ship at sea, your moods—the winds,
The currents moving and the threatening rocks
That guard old fairylands of promises ;
Those pleasant possibilities of Time
When the great seas go down and harbour seems
Of sure attainment, when the racing storm
And mangled foaming have been harvested
By the calm quietude of silent eves.
Then shall you see a port with welcome joy,
And trim the sails, steer on the craft with care.
The weary crew of your imaginings
Grown sceptical with suffering of salt waves
And striving days of stress and storm, now kneels,
And with a fervour got from prayers vouchsafed
Gives thanks to Fate.  Oh false-illusioned souls,
The sanctity of harbour is too short !
You have forgot no ship has any home
Other than tumult ;  battling with the speed
Of the great multitudes and waves of thought,
The drastic hurricanes of huge emotion,
Despairing, long, flat calms of misery
When rowing fails—precipitous heights and deeps
Of wild mid-ocean madness, shifting sands

Where patience runs aground and perishes ;
And yet you deem it freedom ! Life at sea,
Tossed round forever, battered, staggering on
To finish voyages and recommence.
Better maybe at last unstop our ears
And follow the songs of sirens, guilelessly,
Down to the depths of some enchanted death
Where pain has been forgotten, tears shut out,
And old out-grown emotions turned away ;
Where, like a miracle maybe, we'd find
Reflection of the same soft paradise,
Rare as on earth, but now attainable.

# EVENINGS

Now when you hear the musing of a bell
Let loose in summer evenings, mark the poise
Of summer clouds, the mutability
Of pallid twilights from a tower's crest—
When you have loved the last long sentiment
Slipped on-to earth from sunset, seen the stars
Come pale and faltering, the blaze of flowers
Grow dim and grey, and all the stuff of night
Rise up around you almost menacing—
When you have lost the guide of colour, seen
The daylight like a workman trudging home
Oblivious of your thoughts and leaving you
Silent beside the brim of seas grown still,
Placid and strange.   When you have lingered
        there,
And shuddered at the magic of a moon
That will not sleep, but needs your vigilance
And seizes on the musings of your soul
Till you are made fanatical and wild,
Torn with old conflicts and the internal fire
Of passion and love, excessive grief of tears

And all the revolutions found in life—
What then ? your body shall be crucified,
Your spirit tortured, and perhaps found good
Enough a tribute for some ultimate art.

# THE RIVER NENE

OH the eternal sweetness of the river
Under mysterious sunsets, creeping on
Through meadows flowerless and low ; to-day
Sleeping they stretch in silent mellowness.
No April flowers are here, nor butterflies
Trilling on spotted cowslips, for to-day
Nature's communion with the darkening season
Sets amber berries glowing, clustered birds
Whispering in autumn hedgerows.  In the sky
Clouds meditate and slowly pass to westward ;
The velvet greens are smoothed—I have walked long
Illumined by the purity of sunset
Soft as a kiss ; stood on the gentle hills
And wondered at the world, this delicate
Sweet solitude of midland river valley
That wanders as a dream.  I have gone by
The murmurous mill, the greyness of a village,
And loved the vesperal merging of the day
Into completed acquiescent night ;
Found here the long reposeful altitudes
That guide the soul to heavens temporal.

# VOYAGES NORTH

THE strange effects of afternoons !
Hours interminable, melting like honey-drops
In an assemblage of friends . . .
Or jagged, stretching hard unpleasant fingers
As we go by, hurrying through the crowds—
People agape at shops, Regent Street congested
With the intolerable army of winter road-workers
Picking ; then in the Café Royal
Belated drunkards toying with a balloon
Bought from a pedlar—streets and stations
Serried together like cheap print, swinging trains
With conversational travellers arguing on the
    Opera—
Newspapers, agitation of the mind and fingers,
The first breath of country dispelling undue
    meditation
With the reposeful promise of village firesides ;
Greetings at meeting—But if I were free
I would go on, see all the northern continents
Stretch out before me under winter sunsets ;
Look into the psychology
Of Iceland, and plumb the imaginations
Of travellers outlandish, talking and drinking

With stern strange companies of merchants ;
I should learn
More than one could remember, walk through the
　　days
Enjoying the remoteness, and laughing in foreign
　　places ;
I should cure my heart of longing and impatience
And all the penalties of thought-out pleasure,
Those aftermaths of degradation
That come when silly feasts are done.
I should be wise and prodigal, spending these new
　　delights
With the conviction of a millionaire
Made human by imagination—they should be
The important steps that lead to happiness
And independence of the mind ; then should I say
Final farewell to streets of memories,
Forget the analytical introspection
And the subjective drowsiness of mind,
Stamping into the dust all staleness of things out-
　　grown,
Stand on a northern hill-top shouting at the sun !

# THE LOVE STORY

THE time for fairy-tales is past ; secure
The latch was shut on children's dreams, but one
Escaped, and daring fled into the world
Where growing magic'ly, men called it Love . . .
In secret hurrying through the troubled nights
Like feverish criminals that fear pursuit
We hide the gold of our discovery,
Trembling to look on it ; ah, where shall be
Time for the heart to rest and hands to hold
Untrembling all the treasure, breath be found
To conjure into life this stolen gain
And clasp it, willing fellow to our joy ?
The shining bird that will not be constrained
Nor tamed with dazzling toys, the lightning flame
That strikes and shatters, the fiery paradox
That burns the soul into a sobbing sea
When all is done and the sweet story fled ;
Then grow we old, and weary of all tales ! . . .

D

# TRANSMUTATION

THIS transmutation of the visible
Into subconscious feelings of the past,
And the insistence of declining autumn,
Mysterious vapour, latent colouring
Of humid clouds, clouds like a face aghast.
We breathe in memories, and the infinite loss
Of summer—Silences are like dumb grief,
Preying and long, woven with spell of tears
Come from untravelled regions, unexplored
By consciousness ; this an instinctive day,
Dateless but poignant, solemnly subdued—
We are the prisoners of the sky and earth,
The suffering hostages of memory.

# LOVE

OH Love, shall we not leave you at the last !
We have exploited all your mysteries
And lures of glamour ; time's corollary
Is heavy with our vows, our platitudes
Attempting happiness—love that was proud
And tightly clasped the honourable sword
Of disillusion to a passionate breast ;
Adventurous love that would not be gainsaid,
And sought to storm the world with eloquence
Making a hero out of commonplace ;
Or kindly love compassionate as sleep,
Pure as a song of peace, (a charity
That also has been spurned, unrecognised).
For we have suffered as the martyrs, sought
After your revelations secretly,
Trembling yet brave ; we have put out of
    mind
The gaping mockeries of our defeat,
Thinking to climb a summit, dreaming then
To gather up some prize of recompense
In a new world untrammelled with horizon.
But all these roads are circular and dark,

Remote with loneliness, ending in nought
Beyond the cynical smile of memory. . . .

.        .        .        .        .        .

Oh love, must we not leave you at the last !

# POOR-STREETS

THEY shall not know the tuneful words of love
Nor the impatience of imagination ;
They shall not see the meaning of the day,
Nor slip into the comfortable dreams
Of which we make pleased profitable hours.
For they shall plod and shudder in the streets,
Shadowed by poverty's unending sadness ;
Streets that are long and sullen, unrelieved
By smile of sunlight.  Winter is your season
And all your meaning, suburbs ! pale-faced skies
Shall weigh on you as lead—Oh, hideous poor,
Accursed of life, there is no explanation
Of fate incomprehensible ! no clue
That I should sit by a secluded fire
And know the ending of your day will be
The desolate despair of public-houses.

# THE WREATH

LOVE has destroyed my life, and all too long
Have I been enemy with life, too late
Unlocked the secrets of existence ! there
Found but the ashes of a fallen city
Stamped underfoot, the temple of desires
Run through with fire and perished with defeat.
I would not speak the word of Disillusion
But have long felt the seal of melancholy
Stamped on my sombre autumn resignation.
My loves have been voracious, many-coloured,
Fantastic, sober, all-encompassing,
Have flown like summer swallows at the sun
And dipped into a wintry world of water :
Returned with laughing eyes or blenching face
From each horizon, from the Ever-New :
Passed through Adventure's net, struck at the stars
Flung by excitement recklessly so high :
Delved into precipices warily
And picked the jewel there from dragon-jaws :
Questioned the sphinx of Personality
Reading the puzzling riddles of the sand,
Bringing back prizes, bringing home defeat ;
Sometimes to answers ancient questions turned,

Or driven on, flown like unbalanced moths
Round the perpetual candle of a sage,
Dropping to dust on Science's midnight.
They have gone forth like innocent crusaders
To win the ideals of mediævalism ;
They have set sail on roving western waters,
Searched for Eternity in worlds untame,
Fought for their lives against the rush of Time
And known the despairs of death, and war's
    dismay—
Of these my cunning crown is made, of these
Imperious leaves the sombre final wreath !

# SONNET

I HAVE lost faith in symbols, wearily
Put out of mind their virtues stripped by Time ;
Their magic sciences are gone from me,
Lost as a line that halts, a broken rhyme,
Dead as an ancient metre, dumb as thought
That may not be expressed : some tortured theme
That follows like a ghost, from memory brought
By the persistent power of a dream,
Unwanted, all recurrent—Where shall be,
When the last flame is out, solution found,
An explanation of philosophy
For they that live, or lie deep underground ?
Oh, we shall never know, nor they be free—
Unanswered riddles move the world around. . . .

# ANSWER TO A REPROOF

Let my impatience guide you now, I feel
You have not known that glorious discontent
That leads me on : the wandering after dreams
And the long chasing in the labyrinth
Of fancy, and the reckless flight of moods—
You *shall* not prison, shall not grammarise
My swift imagination, nor tie down
My laughing words, my serious words, old thoughts
I may have led you on with, baffling you
Into a pompous state of great confusion.
You have not seen the changing active birds
Nor heard the mocking voices of my thoughts ;
Pedant-philosopher, I challenge you
Sometimes with jests, more often with real things,
And you have failed me, you have suffered too
And struggled, wondering.  The difference lies
In the old bulk of centuries, the way
You have been fashioned this or that ; and I
Belong to neither, I the perfect stranger,
Outcast and outlaw from the rules of life,
True to one law alone, a personal logic
That will not blend with anything, nor bow
Down to the general rules ; inflexible,

And knowing it from old experience ;
So much for argument—*My* trouble is,
It seems, that I have loved a star and tried
To touch it in its progress : tear it down
And own it, claimed a " master's privilege "
Over some matter that was element
And not an object that would fit the palm
Of a possessor, master-mind itself
And active-ardent of its liberty.

We work apart, alone ; conflicting tides
Brim-filled with angers, violences, strife,
Each championing his own idealism,
Romanticism and sceptic bitterness . . .
The last I leave you, for this present mood
(The name of which you have expounded so)
Has turned against you, bared insulting teeth
And snarled away its rage into the smile
Of old remembrance : " You were ever so,"
Exacting and difficult ; in fact the star
That will not, cannot change for all the price
Of love or understanding—mark you *now*
I have concluded we are justified
Each in his scheming ; is this not a world
Proportioned large enough for enemies
Of our calibre ?  Shall we always meet
In endless conflict ?  I have realised

That I shall burn in my own hell alone
And solitarily escape from death ;
That you will wander guideless too, and dream
(Sometimes) of what I *mean*, the things unsaid,
Vacant discussions that have troubled you
And left me desperate as a day of rain.

Then we shall meet at cross-roads in wild hours
Agreeing over fundamental fates,
Calamities of a more general kind
Than our own geniuses have kindled up.
But at the fabulous Judgment-day, the End,
We shall be separate still, and you will find
That Destiny has posted you once more
Back in the sky—and I shall be on earth.

# SONNET

WHAT will you say of me if I should die
Without the last words spoken ?   Shall there be
Some brave religion that will testify
Belief in my strange faith, and bury me
As I would wish ?  with arms upstretched and high
Cold eyes turned seaward, souls symbolical
Caught in a prison still ;  they shall not die
But be mute audience to the logical
Denunciation of my life by you,
You, the calm critics, and the easeful wise
That have long done with doubt and take for true
That which is taught by faith, and seen with eyes,
Learnt from life's lessons—mourners will be few
That follow my last questioning surmise.

# WESTERN ISLANDS

THE islands of the blessed, the sunset isles,
Full of long summer, and the undying light
That pauses in its radiancy ; and there,
The distant piping of some quavering music
That has expressed the lyric souls of gods
And the long loves of heroes—There have I seen
Isolda bearing Tristan on the waves
From rugged melancholy to dreaming death ;
And syren-lovers weaving wreaths of song
Tuned to the tides, while poets slowly dream
The delicate tales of intermingling souls.
Now time breathes death and life, but leads all there
On the last western voyage of the sun,
All that is worthy of infinitude ;
Heroes and lovers made immortal there
By the insistence of undying beauty.
In exultation shall we not approach
This mystic heaven that outstrips the stars ?
And find anew the passions lived on earth,
Yea, without stress, but in beatitude.

# THE HAUNTED CASTLE

OUTSIDE, the staring eye of emptiness,
Eyes of the dead unclosed ! What lovely sin
In long forgotten centuries within
Filled the glad rooms with transient happiness ?
This castle is a husk of flowers dead,
This barren window has enclosed an hour
Saved from the world by love ; alas, no power
Brings back for us these tales, romances sped
Down to the grieving sea, and out beyond
The last red clouds of sunset—empty rooms
Wait for new stories, wait with vacant eyes,
Eyes of the dead ; the waves are ever fond
Of midnight sorrowing, and the castle looms,
Gaunt, without answer to the moon's surmise.

# THAMAR

THAMAR in distant Georgia watched the sun
Set in voluptuous solitude ; the hills
Brought to her lovers, and she bound their wills
Under her own firm spell, and every one
Of pleasure tasted, marvelled, and was dead :
Cast into night after a little hour
Of paradise incarnate, for her power
None might escape, by fate thereunto led.
But in the silent halls where love had lain,
Captive of all her beauty, wisdom, pride,
Rose clamouring ghosts that made her turn aside
Her longing eyes, as yet she waved again,
(Herself now prisoner of the loves that died,)
Signal continuous o'er the endless plain.

The Mayflower
Press

William Brendon & Son Ltd
Plymouth

CPSIA information can be obtained at www.ICGtesting.com
Printed in the USA
LVOW03s0339281114

415888LV00016B/659/P